Berlin Wall

Berlin Wall

Memorial Site, Exhibition Center

and the Chapel of Reconciliation on Bernauer Strasse

Edited by "The Berlin Wall –

Memorial Site and Exhibition Center" Association

Jaron Verlag

Original edition
First printing 1999

Translation: Tom Lampert, Berlin
Cover design: Atelier Kattner, Berlin. Cover photos courtesy of Günter Schneider
(from top to bottom: the demolition of the Church of Reconciliation, 1985;
the Berlin Wall Memorial Site, 1998; the Wall along Bernauer Strasse, 1979 and 1981)
Map on back cover: Gerd O. Gauglitz
Typeset and lithography: LVD GmbH, Berlin
Printed and bound: cayfosa, Industria Gráfica, Barcelona
Printed in Spain

ISBN 3-89773-009-X

Table of Contents

Preface

Gabriele Camphausen

On November 9, 1997, the day the symbolic foundation stone was laid for the monument on the Berlin Wall Memorial Site on Bernauer Strasse, the Senator for Science, Research and Culture in Berlin appointed a group of experts to work out preliminary plans for the development of an exhibition center on the history of the Berlin Wall.

After the necessary groundwork was completed and a conceptual framework for an exhibition center had been worked out, an official association in support of the project was formed from this group of experts. On November 5, 1998, "The Berlin Wall – Memorial Site and Documentation Center" Association was established with its residence in Berlin. The goals of the association are to guide the thematic content of the memorial site, to document and present the history of the Berlin Wall through the example of Bernauer Strasse, and to encourage discussion and analysis of the history and significance of the Wall itself. The opening of an working exhibition has been planned on November 9, 1999, for the tenth anniversary of the fall of the Wall.

This booklet provides an overview of the historical events on Bernauer Strasse. It also presents the plans for the memorial site ensemble on Bernauer Strasse, as well as examining the preparations for the individual elements of this ensemble. Throughout the pamphlet, attention has been paid to the disputes which, from the beginning, have accompanied discussion and work around the memorial site.

The Berlin Wall Memorial Site along the former "death strip" or Todesstreifen on Bernauer Strasse

Understanding the Present by Looking Back at the Past

Bernauer Strasse and the Berlin Wall Memorial Site

Helmut Trotnow

The first unusual feature which visitors today on Bernauer Strasse notice are the cemeteries. There are two of them, one on the left-hand side and one on the right-hand side of Ackerstrasse, the street which connects Bernauer Strasse with the center of the city. One of the cemeteries belongs to the Sophien Parish, the other to the Elisabeth Parish, which is now part of an association of parishes. There are three more cemeteries in the immediate vicinity as well. The concentration of cemeteries in this area is no coincidence. At its inception in the 19th century, Bernauer Strasse lay on the northern outskirts of Berlin, and led, as its name suggests, as an arterial road northeast to the city of Bernau, which is about 30 kilometers away. Historically, cemeteries were always located on the outskirts of cities. Today, this area is itself a part of the city center. From Bernauer Strasse, one can walk to Alexanderplatz via Ackerstrasse in twenty minutes. The Reichstag is not much farther away.

The former city outskirts along Bernauer Strasse assumed a fateful role after the end of the Second World War. When the victorious Allied powers – the Soviet Union, on the one hand, and the Western Powers France, Great Britain and the United States, on the other – organized the occupation of the German Reich's capital city in 1945, they oriented themselves according to the district borders of Greater Berlin as they had existed in 1920. The buildings on the eastern side of Bernauer Strasse were assigned to the district Berlin-Mitte, and thus to the Soviet Sector. The sidewalk, however, lay in the district Berlin-Wedding and was thus a part of West Berlin. As long as freedom of movement was permitted in the city, this was not a problem. However, when the German Democratic Republic (GDR) erected border fortifications in August 1961 in order to halt the migration of its citizens into the Western part of the city, there were dramatic attempts to escape along Bernauer Strasse. Who does not remember the terrifying photographs of people jumping out of windows from the upper stories of buildings, while border police barricaded and later walled in entrances and windows below? Residents sought to escape the hated regime, as it were, at the very last minute. Not everyone succeeded. In the first year after the erection of the Wall alone, seven people died. Crosses and memorial stones were laid in memory of the victims. Later, a proper monument of mourning developed at the upper end of Bernauer Strasse. Today, the crosses have become an historical monument which is now located between the Brandenburg Gate and the Reichstag.

The second unusual feature which visitors on Bernauer Strasse immediately notice are the two large Christian institutions. The Lazarus Hospital and Deaconess House (today simply the Lazarus Hospital) are located diagonally opposite the Nordbahnhof on the left-hand side of the street. In 1870, the facilities were opened through the initiative of the minister Wilhelm Boegehold, and offered medical care to poorer members of Prussian-German society. The first patients were people wounded in the battles for German unification between 1866 to 1870. Over the course of time, the facilities expanded. Next to the hospital, there was also a children's home and a rest home. The organization's activities were focused on the people in the district Berlin-Mitte, although the deaconesses were also active in the surrounding countryside in Brandenburg. With the erection of the border in 1961, however, the organization was compelled to fundamentally reorient itself, as it was cut off from those people whom it had previously served. For the deaconesses, this separation was particularly painful, as the graves of their deceased sisters were located in the cemetery of the Sophien Parish on the other side of the border. Incidentally, the first refugees injured on Bernauer Strasse during escape attempts from the GDR received medical care at the Lazarus hospital.

The second Christian institution on Bernauer Strasse is the Evangelical Reconciliation Parish, which attained sorrowful fame when its church was blown up by the GDR. The image of the collapsing church tower was seen around the world. The parish itself was established in 1894 from the Elisabeth Parish, and was, from the beginning, intensively engaged in social work. In 1902, the Parish established the "Association for the Service of the Unemployed." This association operated a "breadkitchen" on Ackerstrasse, where the homeless and unemployed in Berlin were offered a daily meal in a Christian environment. The location of these two organizations was by no means a coincidence. With the process of industrialization during the 19th century, this area, which would later become the district of Berlin-Wedding, developed into a typical working class neighbourhood with tenement blocks and manufacturing plants. While in 1855, fewer than 8,000 people lived here, there were 25,000 inhabitants with the establishment of the German Reich in 1871. Around the turn of the century, the population had risen to 140,000, and by the beginning of the Second World War, it reached its peak at around 350,000. Not surprisingly, social problems arose with this population explosion. The Lazarus House as well as the Reconciliation Parish sought to alleviate the worst misery of the poor. They did this with the full approval of higher circles in the German Reich. Empress Auguste Victoria was herself present when the Church of Reconciliation was consecrated in 1894. Church and state worked closely together to prevent social developments from getting out of hand in the northern suburb, not far removed from the center of Berlin. These fears were not unfounded. Already in the Kaiserreich, one spoke of "Red Wedding," where the Social Democrats amassed their supporters, as did the Communists during the Weimar Republic. Both political parties pleaded for fundamental changes in Prussian-German class society of the time.

With the construction of the Wall, the parish lost its church, which lay right in the middle of the new border fortifications. Four years later, the parish established a new parish house on Bernauer Strasse, diagonally opposite its old Church. If everything proceeds according to plan, this building will house the Exhibition Center on the history of the Berlin Wall.

The brutal recklessness with which the GDR regime erected its borders is evident in a particularly macabre way in the cemetery of the Sophien Parish. Many famous artists and composers of the 19th century and the beginning of the 20th century, including Albert Lortzing, Carl Bechstein and Walter Kollo, were buried here. With good reason, one spoke here of a "musicians' cemetery." The graves in the back part of the cemetery, however, stood in the way of the construction of the border fortifications and were therefore removed. From photographs and films, we know that there were repeated reburials. However, whether only the gravestones were actually re-located can no longer be determined with certainty for individual cases. The Parish rightfully spoke of a desecration of its cemetery.

It is only with great difficulty that one can imagine today the character which Bernauer Strasse had as a junction between the northern suburb and the city center. Only the green fallow land on the east side of the street today hints at the fact that there were once buildings here. Before the erection of the Wall, there was an active border trade along Bernauer Strasse, particularly at the Bad/Brunnenstrasse intersection. The "border crossers," i.e., those who lived in the Eastern part of the city and worked in the Western part, and who thus had access to hard Western currency, could stock up on those goods which were not available in their own sector. In addition to this, they used the numerous movie theaters in the West to escape the tristesse of Communist society for a few hours. In a single moment, however, this pulsating life came to an end. The once lively thoroughfare became a deserted cul-de-sac pervaded by a ghostly atmosphere. United States President John F. Kennedy might have had Bernauer Strasse in mind when he said in his famous speech in front of Schöneberg City Hall in West Berlin, "Even freely organized societies have their difficulties, and our democracy itself is not perfect. But we never had to wall our people in." Following the building of the Wall, only a few tourists came to Bernauer Strasse to get an impression of the tragedy of a divided city. The wooden observation platform, which stood on the corner of Bernauer Strasse and Ackerstrasse and offered visitors an unimpeded view of the border facilities, has been preserved. After its restoration, one will be able to see it in the Exhibition Center. Bernauer Strasse has remained alive in our memory, for nowhere else along the Berlin Wall were there so many successful escapes to West Berlin. Some of these escapes were downright spectacular and became world-famous. Who does not remember the photograph of the GDR border soldier Conrad Schumann, who jumped to freedom on the corner of Ruppiner and Bernauer Strasse two days after the Wall went up? The photograph has become an icon. Another successful escape took place in October 1964, when 57 people made it from the East to the West through of a tunnel 12 meters deep and more than 150 meters long. The tunnel entrance was located on the eastern side of Strelitzer Strasse, the tunnel exit was on Bernauer

Strasse 97. During the escape, there was an exchange of fire, which ended with the death of a GDR People's Policeman, Egon Schultz. Testimony about such attempted escapes – regardless of whether they were successful or not – was collected and displayed as an exhibition for the first time in October 1962 on Bernauer Strasse. Today, this collection forms the basis for the Museum "House at Checkpoint Charlie."

Given this historical background, it is understandable why, after the opening of the Berlin Wall and the collapse of the Communist GDR regime, the German Historical Museum proposed in the Spring of 1990 that a segment of the Berlin sector border along Bernauer Strasse should be made an historic monument. This was not, as criticisms of the proposal later suggested, a matter of creating an historical adventure park or a "Disneyland." The Berlin Wall, however, should be preserved in its authentic form as it was on November 9, 1989. Willy Brandt was the first person to suggest this. Brandt himself had been the Mayor of West Berlin when the border fortifications were put up, and then went on to become the Chancellor of the Federal Republic and a Nobel Peace Prize winner. In a brief speech on November 10, 1989, in front of Schöneberg City Hall, Brandt suggested that "a piece of that hideous construction be left standing ... in remembrance of an historical monstrosity." The term 'Berlin Wall,' although generally employed, is highly misleading. In the course of its almost 30-year existence, this border continuously changed its appearance. The initial barbed wire was later replaced with stone. The prefabricated wall elements facing west were added at the end of the 1970's and beginning of the 1980's. In addition to this "external border wall" towards the West, there was also an "internal border wall" facing East. Between the two walls there was the so-called "death strip" or Todesstreifen, where people attempting to escape were shot at. In this area, there were watchtowers and lighting systems, signal and alarm fences and facilities for guard dogs. The Wall itself existed as border only between the two parts of Berlin. The rest of the GDR was divided from West Berlin by a metal fence.

The idea of a memorial site proved extremely difficult to realize. The initial opinion of people in Berlin was that the Wall should disappear as quickly as possible. The first spontaneous demolitions began on the night of November 9, 1989. Following this, millions of people from around the world came to Berlin to chip off a piece of this Wall of disgrace – proof that the repression of freedom and democracy was finally over. The part of the Berlin Wall along Bernauer Strasse was regarded as the most profoundly symbolic segment. As a result, the first crossing point from West to East Berlin was opened here. It should be emphasized that the current site of the memorial differs from the original proposal. The German Historical Museum had simply proposed preserving a section of the Wall along Bernauer Strasse. The initial chaotic demolitions of the Wall, however, proceeded so rapidly that officials responsible for the protection of historic monuments could not keep pace. Whenever a section of the Wall along the street was supposed to be placed under protection, it had already been torn down before the resolution could be passed. In the end, only a section approximately 200 meters long on Bernauer Strasse, between Berg- and Ackerstrasse, remained. The original proposal had conceived a memorial site with three elements. The actual Wall monument was supposed to be supplemented by an exhibition center and the reconstruction of the cemetery. The Berlin Senate passed a resolution supporting this idea in 1991, on the occasion of the 30th anniversary of the Wall. What followed was an extremely heated debate, which ended with the monument in its current form. Since the official opening of the monument on August 13, 1998, it has become clear that the history of this border cannot be related to future generations by this monument alone. The proposed exhibition center is absolutely necessary. The questions to answer are clear: Why was the Berlin Wall built, who was responsible for it? How did people on both sides of the border live with the Wall, and what were the causes and consequences of its removal? With the fall of the Berlin Wall, the Cold War ended in Europe. The world, however, has not become a more secure place as a result of this. The fundamental values of freedom and democracy are still threatened today. That is reason enough to keep the historical memory of the Berlin Wall alive.

Barrier wall with tank barricades and visual barriers on Bernauer Strasse at the corner of Schwedter Strasse, October 1963

Willy Brandt, the governing Mayor of Berlin, visits Bernauer Strasse on August 13, 1964, the third anniversary of the building of the Wall

People out on a walk along the Wall on Bernauer Strasse 1969

Monument to Ernst Mundt in front of the modernized Wall border. Taken in front of the Sophien Cemetery on Bernauer Strasse, September 1980

The "death strip" on Bernauer Strasse in front of the Sophien Cemetery, looking in the direction of Gartenstrasse, July 1981

A “Wall-picker” on Bernauer Strasse, December 1989

The official demolition of the inner city Wall in Berlin begins

Opening of the intersection between Bernauer Strasse and Ackerstrasse on July 13, 1990

The Monument on the Berlin Wall Memorial Site

A Process of Development

Gabriele Camphausen

For almost ten years now, there have been controversial discussions about erecting an appropriate memorial on Bernauer Strasse. The contentious question at the center of these debates has been, should there be any kind of permanent memorial dedicated to the history of the Berlin Wall on this location? And if so, what form should this take – should there be an open-air museum or an historical documentation, a monument or a site of remembrance? Questions about the degree to which the Wall itself should be preserved or reconstructed have, in this context, also fueled heated debates. The disputes about the content and structure of a memorial site have taken a number of surprising turns and have been carried out, at least in part, in a bitter tone. Even the inauguration of the monument on the Berlin Wall Memorial Site on August 13, 1998, did not lead to a fundamental easing of tensions or to an end of the discussions. On the contrary, the monument seems to have provided the controversy with a new impetus. If one considers the politically relevant and delicate nature of the subject under discussion here, then the heated atmosphere of the debate is hardly surprising. Why should the decision about the erection of a memorial for the Wall proceed easily and smoothly, when the treatment of recent German history as a whole is difficult and problematic? The struggle to make history understandable for the present stands irreconcilably opposed to the desire to have matters closed once and for all, and to look to the future without having to deal with a painful and unwieldy past. This conflict was evident from the beginning in debates about the construction of a memorial site on Bernauer Strasse, a street which itself has been a crystallization point in East-West German history.

Another controversial aspect of debate has arisen around the recently erected monument itself, namely the question as to what a monument can actually achieve, what knowledge it can impart and what expectations it can fulfill. Discussions about monuments have consistently raised a broad spectrum of very different demands, approaches and proposals, as is evident, for example, with the planned memorial for July 17, 1953, and the memorial for the murdered Jews in Europe. In these two cases, there has been a clear didactic mistrust of artistic attempts to deal with history; indeed, the appropriateness of the medium of art in general for such purposes has been questioned. Profound differences in understanding and opinion among contemporary witnesses, politicians and artists have also emerged, as well as the impression of many people directly affected that they were not adequately included in the decision-making process. In light of these fundamental issues, how could one expect that the different opinions about the monument to the Wall on Bernauer Strasse could be accommodated smoothly and easily?

The monument to the Wall itself, however, was not solely responsible for the vehemence of the discussion. The debate is also a measure of existing historical-philosophical differences within German society, admittedly a very sensitive measure.

Let us look back for a moment at the developments leading up to August 13, 1998, the day on which the monument facilities were officially transferred from the Federal Government to the Land Berlin. Since the fall of the Wall, "Wall-pickers" and "Wall-protectors" have stood opposed to one another. In order to prevent the Wall from completely disappearing, the former GDR Museum for German History, the German Historical Museum and others have struggled to preserve historical material and evidence of the Wall on Bernauer Strasse and have sought to protect dismantled parts of the Wall facilities (watch towers and blockades, lampposts.) They initially received support from municipal authorities in East Berlin, who declared on October 2, 1990, one day before German unification, a 212 meter-long section of the Wall along Bernauer Strasse to be an historic monument. (The Berlin Senate confirmed this registration in its historical monument book in February 1992.)

According to the German Historical Museum's proposal, a memorial site on Bernauer Strasse which combined historical evidence and reconstruction, documentation and remembrance was to be opened on August 13, 1991, the thirty-year anniversary of the erection of the Wall. The reconstruction of the border facilities at the Wall, the opening of an exhibition center, and the erection of a memorial site for the victims of the Wall were planned. The intention was to create a site of silent explanation and remembrance.

From the beginning, however, there was heated opposition to this proposal, for various reasons, from residents, people directly affected and politicians. The neighbouring districts Berlin-Wedding and Berlin-Mitte and, in particular, the Evangelical Sophien Parish and the Deaconess-Hospital "Lazarus" made no secret of their opposition to retaining these historic objects. One had been forced to live with the Wall long enough, they argued, now there should finally be an end to it and all forms of separation should be done away with. In addition to this, the Sophien Parish demanded the return of its cemetery grounds along the Wall, which it had been forced to sell to the GDR. Thus, one side stood opposed to the other. The one side wanted to remove the Wall to make room for a new future, while the other side wanted to preserve the Wall as a necessary sign of remembrance, in memory of the dictatorship and its victims, and as a reminder that even that which is apparently insurmountable can be overcome. Traffic administrators also entered the debate as a third interested party – they intended to expand Bernauer Strasse into a multilane relief road within the framework of the Berlin inner-city thoroughfare or Innenstadtring.

The differences between the two sides were too sharp for the planned exhibition center and monument to be realized. The Berlin Senate did, however, pass a resolution on August 13, 1991, in which the erection of a memorial site was expressly welcomed. In the following months, a coordinating committee worked out a conception which was accepted by all of the participants – the districts Berlin-Wedding and Berlin-Mitte, the Curator for the Land Berlin, the Berlin Senate's Cultural Administration, the German Historical Museum, the Evangelical Reconciliation Parish, the Evangelical Sophien Parish and the Lazarus Hospital. The core of this agreement regarding the 212-meter segment of the Berlin Wall was the following: first, the return of the cemetery grounds which the Sophien Parish had been forced to sell to the GDR; second, the preservation of a 70-meter-long segment of the Wall along Bernauer Strasse, including a reconstruction of the necessary border facilities; and third, the erection of a memorial site with a monument on the remaining 60 meters. An exhibition center, however, was no longer contained in this compromise.

Although the Berlin Senate accepted the ideas of the coordinating committee on February 2, 1993, this proposal also could not be realized. The opposition of the Sophien Parish repeatedly brought the proceedings to a political standstill. One attempted to halt developments through contradictory information about ostensible mass graves from the Second World War, which would be desecrated by a reconstruction of the Wall facilities. In order to end this new conflict, the Land Berlin finally reached an agreement with the Sophien Parish in the Spring of 1994 that a reconstruction of the border facilities would be dropped and that the remains of the Wall would be left as they were. In addition to this, it was agreed that a "memorial site in remembrance of the victims of the Second World War and the victims of the division of Germany" should be erected. Following this agreement, the Federal Government, represented by the German Historical Museum, initiated a competition for the design of a memorial site on Bernauer Strasse in April 1994. The guidelines for the competition read as follows: The 212-meter section of the Berlin Wall will be divided into three segments. The border facilities will be preserved (or reconstructed) in their entirety along a 70-meter segment; the planned monument will be allotted 60 meters; 70 meters will be returned to the Sophien Parish for use as a cemetery.

A total of 259 proposals were submitted to the competition, which was completed in October 1994. The judges awarded no first place prize, but they did choose three second place winners: Bühren and Schulz from Allensbach, Winkler and Thiel from Berlin, and Kohlhoff & Kohlhoff from Stuttgart. The respective proposals differed greatly from one another. Bühren and Schulz left the "death strip" or Todesstreifen largely untouched in their design, abstaining from divisions of any kind, although they did propose to rebuild the historical path to the cemetery. Their motto was: "This site cannot be made into a memorial. This site is one." Winkler and Thiel from Berlin incorporated a 110-meter segment of the border, surrounded by a 15-meter high, semi-transparent barbed-wire fence in their proposal. Kohlhoff & Kohlhoff's design proposed a 70-meter long border strip framed by two lateral facades made of reflective, polished steel. The steel surfaces were supposed to heighten and enhance the atmosphere within the Wall segment. The final decision as to which of the second place design proposals would be realized now lay in the hands of the competition's sponsor, the Federal Government, which decided in July 1995 for the design proposal of Kohlhoff & Kohlhoff, whose "short" Wall segment also found approval from the Sophien Parish.

The project appeared ready to proceed. Once again, however, things developed differently than had been expected. Contentious questions about financing the memorial initially caused delays. After the Federal Government had finally approved 2.2 million German Marks at the beginning of April 1997, building authorities in the district Berlin-Mitte and the Sophien Parish completely altered the situation by suddenly removing 32 segments of the Wall in order to "protect mass graves located there." The Wall now existed as an original object of East-West German post-war history only in broken fragments.

This demolition, however, seemed to cause a number of people to re-evaluate their position. Earlier, the interest in maintaining the Wall had been minimal, which in part had encouraged the most recent demolition. After April 1997, an increasing number of voices stressed the necessity of preserving as much material evidence of the Wall as possible. Despite the fact that Kohlhoff and Kohlhoff's winning design had proposed only a "small" memorial, the Berlin Senate passed a resolution at the beginning of August 1997 which proposed, in addition to a monument, the reconstruction of the Wall along Bernauer Strasse and the development of an exhibition center.

On November 9, 1997, the construction of the monument according to Kohlhoff & Kohlhoff's proposal began. On August 13, 1998, the Berlin Wall Memorial Site was officially opened, and transferred from the Federal Government to the Land Berlin.

However, this was by no means the end of the disputes about the memorial site. Shortly before the transfer to the Land Berlin, there was a heated debate about the inscription on the monument plaque. The formulation "In memory of the division of the city from August 13, 1961 to November 9, 1989, and in remembrance of the victims of Communist tyranny" was finally agreed upon. Thus, the conflict continued even during the official opening. Contemporary witnesses and concerned associations sharply criticized the form of the monument itself, both the alienation of the artistic rendition of the Wall and the lack of an overall reconstruction true to scale. The monument, it was said, could not recreate the terror of the Wall, or the brutality of the border facilities and the border regime. They argued that it was merely a harmless reflection, in which the historical reality of the Wall was lost.

It is clear that the ideas and opinions of many people – in particular, people directly affected, people with their own painful experiences of the border regime – deviate sharply from the memorial plans which are currently being realized. These tensions, however, can neither be avoided nor resolved, however much one might try. Just as personal experience and memory encompass a broad spectrum of forms and content, the expectations of remembrance and commemoration, too, are broad and contradictory. There is not one formulation for a true and correct commemoration.

Thus, the monument on the Berlin Wall Memorial Site cannot achieve everything that is expected and demanded of it. It cannot bring the terror of the past back to life, nor can it reflect the different human experiences true to scale, nor even explain the historical-political context. It cannot, above all, correct the mistakes which have been made since 1989 regarding the preservation of historical evidence and regarding the discussions about the injustice which people have suffered. A monument can, however, stimulate interest, it can shake people out of their everyday routine, and make them stop and think. But it cannot actually provide information – for this, other forms of remembrance are necessary.

As a result of contradictory planning, the Wall Memorial on Bernauer Strasse is currently a solitary monument without any kind of substantive supplement. It has been left to stand alone, as the accompanying exhibition center was, for a time, regarded as unnecessary.

Only beginning in the summer of 1997 did the Berlin Senate again take up the idea of such a center. As a result of this decision, the monument itself is currently overburdened by the expectations and desires of visitors for information. The necessity of expanding the Berlin Wall Memorial Site into an ensemble with an exhibition center is more evident today than ever.

Action "Wall-Land Lupin." Citizens of the GDR plant lupin seeds along the former "death strip" on Bernauer Strasse in the Summer of 1990

The grounds of the Berlin Wall Memorial Site in the Summer of 1991

A view of the external border wall, which was supposed to be protected as an historical monument, but was damaged in the Spring of 1990 by two demolitions. In the foreground, the access road along the former Sector border

Dismantled Wall segments on the grounds of the Sophien Cemetery, 1997

The opening of the Berlin Wall Memorial Site on August 13, 1998. From the left: Dr. Klaus-Peter Eich, a victim of the Wall, Federal Environmental Minister Dr. Angela Merkel, Provost Dr. Heinrich Lüdtke, Berlin Mayor Eberhard Diepgen

Design proposal for the Wall monument by the architects Kohlhoff and Kohlhoff from Stuttgart

A view of the back of Berlin Wall Memorial Site, photographed from the cemetery of the Sophien Parish

View through an observation slit of the internal border wall on the Memorial Site

The Berlin Wall Exhibition Center

Gabriele Camphausen

Ten years after the fall of the Berlin Wall, there are still numerous questions and issues regarding the history of the Wall which remain unresolved. Many aspects still require a thorough investigation, and fundamental decisions still have to be made and then realized. This is particularly true of Bernauer Strasse, which for years has been the center of vehement discussions about how to deal with the past. The points of orientation, however, have become clearer over time, and the planning and conceptual preparations for a memorial here have moved forward. The current goal is to create a memorial site ensemble on Bernauer Strasse which will make the historical location here both recognizable and powerfully expressive.

The overall facilities of this planned ensemble to document and commemorate the Berlin Wall consist of several elements. There is a section of the Wall itself as historical evidence, combined with an artistic monument. There is the new Chapel of Reconciliation, built on the location of the former Church of Reconciliation which was blown up in 1985 by GDR border troops. And there is the planned Exhibition Center on the history of the Wall, including historical stations located outside of the memorial site along Bernauer Strasse which deal with the local history here.

These very different elements present an unusual combination, both in their distinctiveness and in their relation to one another. Together, they will provide an introduction to the history of the Wall, on different level and in different forms. The various forms and media used in the memorial site ensemble will provide visitors with a broad spectrum of ways to confront the past. Visitors will be able to choose for themselves the medium of information which they prefer to explore, as well as the level and depth of that information. Among the different media available at the memorial will be the historical site itself, the artistic confrontation with the site, textual and photographic documents about the general political history as well as about the fate of individual people, interactive computer stations, the visual presentation of topics through films, photographs and slides, and acoustic presentations through contemporary recordings and reports from contemporary witnesses. The placement of the individual programs and their concrete historical connections are extremely important: visitors will be able to organize their own encounter with the memorial site, to seek out information that interests them without getting lost in a potpourri of random facts.

The Exhibition Center will be housed in the parish house of the Reconciliation Parish.

Within the memorial site ensemble, this center will fulfill the important function of providing visitors with information. The historical background as well as historical-political developments will be available to visitors in a comprehensible form, encouraging them to engage intensively and individually with the past. The different approaches to this history will be supported through a multiplicity of materials (texts, photographs, films, audio recordings and original objects), and a diversity of forms (exhibition tables, display cases, multimedia information programs.) The digitalization of the Exhibition Center's archive, which is planned for the long-term, will make selected materials available over the Internet, insofar as current privacy laws permit this.

The developments on and around Bernauer Strasse stand at the center of the documentation of the Berlin Wall here, that is, Bernauer Strasse itself forms the concrete historical reference point for the Exhibition Center. Yet, in addition to this, the larger political context will also be presented, for only within this context can the history of Bernauer Strasse be understood. The Exhibition Center is not simply concerned with understanding events from a local perspective, from the perspective of Berliners, or of Germans, or even East and West Germans, but rather with understanding the international frame of reference and the connections between local history with larger political events as well.

Another specific accent of the Exhibition Center will be the connection between public-political history and private-personal experience. Bernauer Strasse remains a focal point of postwar political history, a history which was experienced both on a governmental-political level and on private-human one. In erecting a closed border through the middle of an established residential street, the brutal consequences of the division of Germany were immediately evident and palpable. Life paths and human relationships were separated overnight. In this context, the tension between the "stabilization" into completely separate political blocks, on the one hand, and individual experiences of suffering through this separation, on the other, is almost impossible to resolve, and forms an extremely difficult chapter of German history.

The future Exhibition Center will be oriented around four key elements: the external and internal time-lines (a chronicle of general political events and a chronicle of the Wall itself), selected in-depth topics, original historical objects, and the development of the area outside the memorial site along Bernauer Strasse.

The external and internal time-lines will offer visitors the necessary historical background and basic knowledge. The external timeline will provide fundamental information about the political emergence and the conditions of development surrounding the Berlin Wall. Among the topics included are the consequences of the Second World War, the Cold War and its effects, particularly in Berlin (the Berlin Blockade of 1948/49, the Berlin Ultimatum of 1958, the Vienna Convention in 1961, espionage, abductions and kidnappings in West Berlin), the increasing political and economic difficulties of the GDR, the building of the Wall, the reactions of the Federal Government and Western powers, the Passage Agreement from 1963 to 1966, the gradual 'normalization,' the era of Détente (the Four-

Power Agreement of 1971, Basic Relations Agreement of 1972, etc.), Perestroika in the Soviet Union and the collapse of the East Block.

An internal time-line, which will be closely correlated with the external time-line, focuses directly on events concerning the Wall itself, in particular along Bernauer Strasse. The index of this internal time-line will range from topics such as the increasing tide of refugees from the East Sector, Ulbricht's statement "No one intends to build a wall," the erection of barbed wire and walled border facilities, and the devastating effects of such a border, to the decision in June 1990 to tear the Wall down (beginning on Bernauer Strasse) and the eventful beginnings of the Berlin Wall Memorial Site.

Supplementary programs focussing on key topics in greater detail will be offered at in-depth stations in the form of multi-media columns, slide shows and films, and audio presentations. These stations will form a counterpoint to the more traditional and sober time-lines.

Intended topics of the electronic presentations will include the following issues: refugees and their fate, the mass escape of 57 people in 1964 through the "tunnel of 57" in Bernauer Strasse 97, acts of resistance such as those organized by Zutshi in 1962, Bernauer Strasse between destruction and survival after the erection of the Wall, the effects of the Wall on church and parish life in Bernauer Straße, the theme "large-scale politics – private-personal experience" in the context of the Wall, the different representations of the Wall in the media, from the "anti-fascist wall of protection" to the "wall of shame," and finally the border regime itself.

The information which can be called up at computer stations will also be supplemented with audio and visual material. Slide shows and film projections will contain sequences of earlier television reports from both East and West Germany about escape attempts and acts of resistance, will report on the construction and alterations of the Wall, about the disappearance of the Wall after 1989, and about controversial questions concerning Germany's divided history and the new life together. Audio stations have been planned which will make available original radio reports about escapes by refugees and about resistance, thus presenting the past in a condensed form. Memoirs from contemporary witnesses will also be used here. Such contemporary recordings and personal accounts of experiences can bring us closer to the past and help us to understand those dimensions of history which would otherwise be forgotten or remain incomprehensible to us.

Original objects and materials concerned with the history of the Wall on Bernauer Straße will form the third key element of the Exhibition Center. Only a small number of authentic items are currently available, but these possess enormous expressive power as material evidence of this history. Research for further items, as well as for private keepsakes must continue.

In order to incorporate and develop the area outside the memorial site, historical stations have been planned along Bernauer Strasse. Information plaques and audio tours will encourage visitors to explore Bernauer Strasse on their own. These historical stations will offer a compact overview of the history of Bernauer Strasse and the Wall border here, and, in addition to this, will provide more detailed information at selected locations. The goal is to present the history in papable form here by providing visitors with an impression of the historical grounds along Bernauer Strasse, which will help them to imagine or remember places and buildings which no longer exist, those sites of everyday life which have been effaced over time. These stations will include, for example, the escape of Conrad Schumann, the GDR People's Policeman, on August 15, 1961, from Bernauer Strasse 37 at the corner of Ruppiner Strasse, the fatal escape attempt of Ida Siekmann from a window in the house on Bernauer Strasse 48 on August 22, 1961, the final escape attempt on the corner of Bernauer Strasse and Brunnenstrasse in 1979, and the demolition of the Church of Reconciliation on Bernauer Strasse 4 on January 22 and 28, 1985.

The development of the Exhibition Center has only just begun. Much is still in the planning stages, and important questions about financing still need to be resolved. Yet the necessity of the Exhibition Center for the history of the Wall is indisputable. If, in the mid 1990's, an exhibition center was not generally regarded as something necessary, it has become clear since then that the Wall must be accepted as a part of East-West German history and must be preserved in the public memory. The actual remains of the Wall are extremely rudimentary, and the memory of the Wall itself continues to fade. Many young people and visitors have no direct reference points to the history of the Berlin Wall. To prevent the disappearance of the Wall from our collective memory, it is absolutely necessary that we document of the past and can provide generally comprehensible historical knowledge and factual information about the Wall. We are faced, then, with the challenge of cultivating and caring for our historical traditions and with confronting the difficult questions of German history. This is a challenge which both Berlin, as an historical location and as the new capital city, and the Federal Republic of Germany as a whole, must meet.

Just as the Wall occupies an indisputable place in Berlin's history, the Exhibition Center here must become an important element among Berlin's documentation and memorial sites. The thematic connections with other historical locations are unmistakable, for example, with the memorial site for the refugee transit camp Marienfelde, with House No.1 in the Normannenstrasse, and with the memorial site Berlin-Hohenschönhausen in the Stasi's former central detention center. All of these locations are necessary, for in their entirety and in their mutual support of one another, they provide a complex image of our recent history and, in doing so, help to maintain our social capacity to remember.

August 1961. Escape from the East Sector through a window. The sidewalk in front of this house on Bernauer Strasse is a part of West Berlin

77-year-old Frieda Schulze escapes from her apartment on Bernauer Strasse in September 1961. GDR People's Policemen attempt to hold her back. Courageous West-Berliners pull her onto the safety sheet of the West Berlin fire department

GDR Soldier Conrad Schumann escapes to West Berlin from Bernauer Strasse at the corner of Ruppiner Strasse on August 15, 1961

▷ Ida Siekmann jumped to her death from this house on Bernauer Strasse 48 onto the sidewalk in West Berlin. Shortly thereafter, the windows of the house were walled in. The houses on the border were later torn down

57 people are able to escape from East Berlin through a tunnel beginning on Strelitzer Strasse 55 on October 3–4, 1964. The tunnel ends in the basement of this house on Bernauer Strasse 97

48

The History of the "Chapel of Reconciliation"

Manfred Fischer

The image of the Church of Reconciliation's collapsing tower was seen throughout the world. First the nave, and then the tower of the old Church of Reconciliation were blown up on January 22 and 28, 1985. With the destruction of the church, the GDR's national security "measures" for object number 7 "concerning the execution of construction requirements necessary for raising the security, order and integrity of the national border to West Berlin" were completed. After 24 years of construction and improvements, after the expulsion of people from their apartments, after the demolition of houses and the erection of supporting wall elements (Type UL 12.41)[1], the border segment Bernauer Strasse was, from the perspective of the GDR rulers, "secure and integral."

In a report on the state of the nation in a divided Germany on February 28, 1985, Federal Chancellor Helmut Kohl said, "This event is a 'symbol.' The demolition of the church shows us how long, how difficult and how uncertain the path before us is in order to overcome the division of Europe and the division of Germany."

For the members of the Reconciliation Parish, the destruction of the Church signified, on the contrary, a profound experience of powerlessness. Whoever experiences this kind of powerlessness is made to feel small and insignificant. He is reminded that he can do nothing, that he is subject to the desires of those more powerful. The only opposition left to him is the symbolic act. With a "dance on the Wall," the Parish bade farewell to its church. In a "Wall-speech," it was said at the time: "We can do something. And if we have faith in symbolic actions, then we know that symbols have a silent power which can make the 'impossible' possible." A few years later, on June 13, 1990, the official demolition of the Berlin Wall began with the removal of a piece of the Wall in precisely this segment of the border along Bernauer Strasse.

When symbols are spoken about in such different ways, it is important to clarify the meaning of the term.[2] The word symbol has a clear theological meaning: religious creed or belief. Every church building is, in this sense, symbolic, for the way in which the pulpit and the alter, the baptismal front and the pews are arranged reflects central questions about a particular religious denomination's form of belief. There are, in addition to this, a multiplicity of less clear meanings of the word, both within theology and outside of it. If one calls the demolition of a church a symbol, then one is using one of these unclear meanings. Something "significant" occurred when the tower collapsed into itself. Was it defeat, or being forced to bid farewell to something familiar, to habits of thought, for example, about the Christian community, whose errors one must learn to recognize when they cannot stand up to history? Or that it might be more appropriate to come together in a modest, simple space? The intact church should also mean something, should be symbolic in this less clear meaning of the term. But not only is the meaning of the word unclear, that which is symbolizes is unclear as well. Was does it mean that Gothic church was built in the 19th century, in a working-class district? Symbols are a matter of feeling, it requires intuition in order to understand them. In the neo-Gothic, romantic emotion resonates, there is the aesthetic of the sublime, the overpowering, as well as nostalgia, the yearning for the clear relations of the village church, which one discovers the first time one looks out of the houses, and the glory of the highest which shines between the modest dwellings. On the other hand, there is the neo-Gothic belief that one can treat one's own history like a storeroom of props that can be used at will. Since 1961, the church has stood directly on the "death strip" or Todesstreifen of the Berlin Wall, less a symbol of reconciliation than of the impossibility of reconciliation. One can also say that the Church of Reconciliation became a symbol the moment its Parish members had to cross the sector border in order to enter church property. The 20th century, however, has found its symbols not in the building of churches, but in their destruction. And that one can see a symbol in the demolition of a church is itself again a metaphor for the destructive character of this century.

The demolition was supposed to create a free field of fire. But it was also supposed to do more than this. An image was supposed to be destroyed. The church, which was literally walled-in by the border, and which, in addition to this, bore the name "reconciliation," exposed the lie of erecting the Wall as "an antifascist wall of protection." But the act which was supposed to erase this image from consciousness produced another image in the consciousness of the international public. The demolition of the church revealed the character of that system even more clearly than the strangulation of the church building through wall and barbed wire had. Instead of being over quickly, of having the horror replaced by peace at the end, the film of the fall is "shown" over and over again, up to the present day. The removal of traces itself leaves behind traces, and these traces are sometimes marked even more clearly in our memory than the original ones were. But the image of the falling church should not be the final image of the Reconciliation Parish.

After the fall of the Wall, the Reconciliation Parish immediately began to look into its own history and tradition. The re-tracing of the history of the Parish before the erection of the Wall was impeded by the fact that with the Wall, the Parish had been limited to West Berlin, while the Parish archive remained in East Berlin, its contents scattered over the years in different places. When this history was finally reconstructed, it became clear that the fate of the Parish itself reflected that of Germany as a whole:

The Evangelical Reconciliation Parish was established in 1894. At this time, Berlin was the largest industrial center in Europe. Wilhelmian Germany flourished in style here. Thousands of people streamed to the new capital city. They sought work, needed a new home. Poverty was widespread. The mission of the newly established parish was a reconciliation of social tensions.

The two World Wars had serious consequences for Germany as well as for the church community. In 1945, Berlin lay in rubble and ashes.

Postwar Germany had a difficult legacy to bear. In Berlin, the "Trümmerfrauen"[3] enabled the reconstruction of the city. The damaged Church of Reconciliation, too, was repaired. But then the city was divided. The border passed right through the middle of the Reconciliation Parish. The mission of the parish on Bernauer Strasse, however, remained reconciliation, a reconciliation which extended beyond political borders.

In 1989, the Wall fell in Berlin. Europe continues to grow together, East and West. What does reconciliation mean today?

The remains of the old church were gradually discovered – a pew, the altar, the church bells, the statue of Jesus Christ, the fallen tower cross. Finally, the old church foundations were exposed. After the property upon which the Wall stood was returned to the Parish, the question arose as to how it should be used in the coming millennium, what the form and content of that use should be. The Parish was aware of the significance of its location through many conversations with old Berliners as well as with young foreign guests of the city – its location on Bernauer Strasse, on the former "death strip," on the foundations of the demolished Church of Reconciliation, on the Berlin Wall Memorial Site.

With this in mind, the Parish formulated a simple mission: that the rescued bells and the altar of the old church should be put to use at their original location. Where could there be a more fitting place to establish a "Chapel of Reconciliation" as an international sign of gratitude for overcoming of the division of Berlin, and the separation of Germany and Europe?

1 These supporting wall elements – painted and then, beginning in 1989, broken off as souvenirs – were, and are still regarded in the public consciousness as the "Wall." This, however, fails to appreciate that the "Wall" was actually a broad, staggered border installation

2 Rolf Engelbart, "Versöhnung von außen und innen," in: 100 Jahre Versöhnungskirche (Berlin, 1994)

3 Literally "rubble women," those women who helped to clear away debris in Germany directly after World War II.

The Design of the "Chapel of Reconciliation"

Manfred Fischer

The design by architects Rudolf Reitermann and Peter Sassenroth creates a chapel appropriate for an urban setting, while, at the same time, constructing an interior space for church services.

The Site

It is important that the particularity of this location be preserved. Despite the consolidation of space for the new Parish quarters, the foundations of the demolished Church of Reconciliation will remain untouched. The new chapel will overlap the old foundations only in the chancel. This open area will provide the church with a spatial distance from the surrounding city. The foundations of the old Church of Reconciliation will also be made visible again. 'Windows,' through which the exposed parts of the historical church foundation can be seen, will be placed in the ground. A room for the church bells will be built in the entrance area – adjoining the old church foundations – behind the returned Christ statue of the demolished church tower. In this room, the old church bells will be hung again on a simple bell trestle.

The Chapel

The interior of the chapel will be reduced to a minimum of indispensable elements, which will serve for contemplation, worship and the communal observation of church services. The goal here is not to create a multipurpose room, but a religious location on the former "death strip" of the Berlin Wall.

The oval ground plan, which faces east, was derived from the circular assembly form. The altar, which was rescued from the old church, will be returned to its original location. The altar table, however, will be reoriented to the East. The new chancel emerges from the oval curve behind the altar table. The altarpiece, pushed into an alcove outside the oval, will retain the alignment of the old church – at right angles to the street. These two axes and the size of the altar will determine the orientation and volume of the church interior. The new building itself will be constructed from bare pounded clay walls 60 centimeters thick. This material was chosen because clay and clay mixtures can satisfy both ecological and construction concerns in an almost ideal way. Pounded clay has been used throughout the world as a building material for thousands of years. It is regarded as the most solid, structurally stable and durable way to build with clay.

A shell will extend over this center area, surrounding the main room as a covered walk, and will form a transition and threshold between the 'outside world' and the religious interior. This external shell, including the roof, will be constructed from wood. The wooden staves of the shell construct a light, translucent cover, which forms a contrast to the massive clay walls of the interior.

The new site for church services must do justice to the altered situation of the parish and its liturgical needs. As an actual site of German history, the "Chapel of Reconciliation" will have effects far beyond the Reconciliation Parish itself.

The "Chapel of Reconciliation" in the Context of the Berlin Wall Memorial Site

Peter C. Bloth

In addition to the concrete and visible artistic rendition of the Wall and the historically oriented Exhibition Center, the "Chapel of Reconciliation" will also form a part of the overall Berlin Wall Memorial Site. This does not mean, however, that the confrontation with terror here presumes a reconciliatory superstructure, an "ultimate" or religious positivity! This will be a place where people, whose personal and spiritual lives, whose social existence as parish was once painfully and destructively disrupted by the Wall, will attempt to explore the ways in which they have dealt with all of those things that constrict openness and freedom.

"Chapel": this was initially the place in which the legendary cape or "cappa" of the holy Martinus was safeguarded in the court of the Frankish Kings. Later, court and palatinate chapels were that part of a building in which relics and other precious objects were kept. One could say that the less a chapel possessed the full legal standing of a parish or a parochial church according to canon law, the greater the essential significance of a room of silence, of contemplation and self-contemplation, of the confronting and attempting to answer the central questions of life became.

Since time immemorial, chapels have been the site of special and spiritual remembrance in Christian culture, whether it be the remembrance of special people or "holy men," or of significant events and occurrences. Thus, only seldom do chapels stand on market places, in the center of hustle and bustle. Even when they are housed under the same roof as a cathedral, chapels are, so to speak, the cathedral's opposite. In its external appearance, the cathedral dome emphasizes the permanence of the bishop's clerical office and its mission of orienting an entire city or society according to justified belief and a decisive ethos. Chapels, on the contrary, provide space for something more intimate – be it in happiness or in doubt – for more personally motivated forms of piety.

If one speaks of chapels in this sense, one can recognize a slogan of modernity, that "religion is a private matter" – admittedly used here in an historically different, i.e. in a political sense. For a chapel within the entire Wall Memorial, however, this social and political dimension of religious life cannot be ignored. The preservation of our communal being against both external and internal subjugation, together with the documentation of that which is indispensable for this, must not be isolated from religion. Nor, conversely, can religion allow itself to be isolated here as well. Thus, the most important thought in planning a "Chapel of Reconciliation" is how "remembrance" and "documentation" can be transcended, or rather, bound together into a Trias, in which publicness and introspection, social life and religious-spiritual life do not remain opposed to one another.

The Evangelical Reconciliation Parish will allow the Berlin Wall Exhibition Center to use its parish house on Bernauer Strasse 111. The Parish will erect a new "Chapel of Reconciliation" on the site of its old "Church of Reconciliation," which, both in its location and its name, stood in the way of building the Wall, and was demolished by the GDR in 1985. Following the wishes of both the Parish and the regional church, this new chapel will no longer stand in the way, but will now lead the way. It will draw people into this special location and invite them to reflect on its meaning in their own personal ways, between the sight of the Wall and the impression of the documents. The oval room, which will be open at all times, should not convey the mythical seclusion of a falsely understood religious nook. The architectural form and the liturgical events here are far more concerned with a kind of "enclosure" of reconciliation for that which has just occurred, as well as for everything which visitors to the Berlin Wall Memorial Site bring with them from their own lives.

What does "reconciliation" mean here? Christian belief attests to the fact that reconciliation is more than, and different from tolerance. With reconciliation, one doesn't simply "let things slide," and particularly not when confronted with brutality and contempt for human life. Reconciliation, rather, strives to make valid and visible how God's actions in his sacrificed and living son Jesus Christ have definitively worked to benefit humanity everywhere in the world – that is what ecumenical means! Every wall of unfreedom, every form of contempt for human dignity falls short of that which, according to God's will, should determine human life. Thus, the word reconciliation, encompassing both the actions of God and those of humans, is not only appropriate in describing the engagement of this church parish on the Berlin Wall, but it can also demonstrate what the church has to offer all individuals, the directions and forms in which it can accompany them in the world today.

With this in mind, the Parish would like to build its "Chapel of Reconciliation" as a part of the overall ensemble of the Berlin Wall Memorial Site, and, in this way, fill its chapel with life. The chapel should be open, and through meditative music should beckon not only to the numerous visitors of the memorial site and the information center, but to all those individuals who seek peace and contemplation today in a world which so often appears cold and harried. Finally, the chapel should also serve as a site of daily prayer for the parish itself, which, on the foundations of its old "Church of Reconciliation," will seek to ensure itself of God's reconciliation with humanity.

The form of the building should also accord with this function: not a grand, cathedral-like structure, not fired bricks or reinforced concrete as a sign of the eternity which humans attempt to create for their 'church' – that has all proved to be, as one can see on Bernauer Strasse, so very embarrassingly fragile. No, the external of wood and the walls of pounded clay should house only the modest and transitory "relics," those remains of the demolished Reconciliation Church – the altar, the bent tower cross. Thus it is, in fact, appropriate that one think of the cape which the holy Martinus once shared with a beggar, so as to provide this homeless man with something with which he could cover himself, and in which he could find warmth in a cold world. For it is the conviction of the Church Parish on Bernauer Strasse that such an act will initiate a process of "reconciliation" appropriate for the present day.

According to this spiritual and parochial conception for the new "Chapel of Reconciliation," the dimensions of introspection and publicness should come together here. As there are no existing models for realizing such an encounter in both church services and forms of daily meditation, this project still requires much reflection by the Parish.

The demolition of the Parish House of the Reconciliation Parish in September 1965

The Church of Reconciliation, no longer accessible, on the “death strip” of the border facilities

The bells of the Church of Reconciliation were taken away by GDR Border Soldiers along Ackerstrasse in January 1985, shortly before the demolition of the church

The demolition of the Church of Reconciliation was announced one day before it began

January 22, 1985: The church nave is blown up

January 28, 1985: The tower of the Church of Reconciliation is blown up

The interior of the Church of Reconciliation before 1945

A model of the “Chapel of Reconciliation” to be build on the foundations of the demolished Church of Reconciliation

In the Spirit of Gandhi

How the Indian Citizen Tapeshwar Nath Zutshi Fought Against the Wall

Doris Liebermann

"The Allgemeiner Deutscher Nachrichtendienst learned that T. N. Zutshi was admitted to a hospital on March 25, because his behavior had raised suspicions that he was mentally disturbed. In addition to this, it was necessary in the interests of public health to determine whether Zutshi was suffering from any infectious diseases. After a thorough medical examination, the patient was released according to his wishes to West Germany in order to take up residence with friends there."[4]

This press release by the Allgemeiner Deutscher Nachrichtendienst on April 1, 1960 was not intended as an April fool's joke. The Indian citizen Tapeshwar Nath Zutshi's peaceful, nonviolent but stubborn protests against the division of Berlin, Europe and the entire world were explained here by the East German authorities as the actions of a mentally disturbed person suspected of being infected with smallpox. Four days earlier, East Berlin radio had reported that Zutshi's actions were "a provocation directed from Schöneberg City Hall in West Berlin."[5] But now it appeared preferable that Zutshi's actions not cause a political sensation in East Berlin.

Zutshi was doubtless aware of what awaited him as he rode the suburban railway (or S-Bahn) on March 26, 1960 into the East Sector of Berlin and got off at Alexanderplatz. He had hung a large cardboard sign around his neck, which read "People behind the Iron Curtain! The first step to freedom is 'Give up your fear and speak the truth.'" Two East German People's Policemen awaited him at Alexanderplatz. They tore the sign from around his neck and led him away.

After five days of imprisonment and interrogation, after admission to a hospital – during which he was made the tempting offer of a sanatorium stay in Switzerland if he would become an advocate of Communist ideology (a heart and liver ailment were ostensibly diagnosed during his arrest) –, after the intervention of the Indian General Consulate in West Berlin through the Yugoslavian Embassy in East Berlin,[6] and after protests from the Social Democratic Party in West Berlin under the leadership of Willy Brandt, Zutshi was finally transported by GDR officials to the border control point at Marienborn, where he was released on foot in the direction of Helmstedt in the Federal Republic of Germany. From there, Zutshi returned to West Berlin.

Between 1958 and 1964, Zutshi repeatedly made headlines in the (West) German press with similar actions. Described as calm and restrained, Zutshi worked in the spirit of Gandhi. He had studied in Benares and at the University of Kansas in the United States, receiving degrees in engineering, chemistry and psychology.[7] Following the Communist occupation of South Korea in 1950, he had apparently resolved to become involved wherever people were threatened with injustice and violence.

With this in mind, Zutshi wrote to Walter Ulbricht in 1960: "As a representative of Russian-Communist imperialism in Eastern Europe, you know that your puppet regime cannot survive without the support of the Russian army."[8] Zutshi's mission led him through Afghanistan to Europe, where, two years after the defeat of the Hungarian uprising by the Soviet military in 1956, Zutshi organized a pilgrimage of 300 Hungarians and Austrians in October 1958 to the Austro-Hungarian border, where they fasted for a week. Zutshi's next stop was Berlin, where he founded the "Satyagraha Society" on Friedbergstrasse 43 in Charlottenburg, in the apartment of his 70-year-old landlady and loyal supporter Charlotte Treichel. According to Zutshi, the mission of this society was to "secure the freedom of West Berlin through nonviolent resistance."[9] He described his own goals as follows:

"First, I did not come to Berlin as a citizen of India, but as a citizen of the world. As such, I, too, belong here and take a deep interest in the fate of this city. Second, I did not come here in order to preach the teachings of Gandhi or nonviolence. I do not feel that I am in a position to do this. However, I do believe that the methods of nonviolence can be used to protect the freedom of West Berlin and, at the same time, to strengthen the spirit of the inhabitants of this city. I believe that we should attempt to use the methods of nonviolence, for this is the only way in which we can exert our influence."[10]

The first action of the "Satyagraha Society" was a three-week fast for freedom in the fall of 1959 at the Brandenburg Gate, combined with the collection of "freedom pledges." In August 1960, Zutshi presented 10,000 signatures to the West Berlin Executive Civil Servant Schulz. Zutshi, however, was not simply a naive dreamer who ignored the political realities of the Cold War. He was well aware of international power relations and was familiar with the work of the United Nations and governments, as well as that of political parties and churches. But he also believed that, in addition to this, the engagement of every individual was necessary as well in order to unify Germany and to push back Soviet influence in Central Europe. Zutshi did not want his work to be understood as "passive resistance," but rather as dynamic and revolutionary action. "When a great number of people have a positive effect on an individual level, a lot can be achieved."[11]

Zutshi was greatly influenced by Mahatma Gandhi, although he did not feel himself unconditionally bound to Gandhi's teachings. While working in South Africa, Gandhi had coined the word "Satyagraha" from the two Sanskrit concepts, "Satya" (truth) and "Agraha" (power or strength). One interpretation of the term "Satyagraha" might be "power of the soul." With this power, Gandhi motivated and led his Indian fellow compatriots to civil disobedience against British colonial rule. Zutshi operated in Berlin according to Gandhi's example:

"Berlin has no military armed forces and is dependent upon foreign powers for its defense. If it is good that foreign powers guarantee Berlin's freedom, it is not good for Berlin to be completely dependent upon them. In any case, it cannot be detrimental if the inner spirit of Berlin receives new power, and if preparations for a nonviolent defense are created. It is a mistake to believe that Satyagraha, understood in the tradition of Gandhi, is a sign of weakness. On the contrary, Satyagraha provides strength and self-confidence ...

The current danger is not that the Russian Army will march into Berlin. The Communists would probably like to make Berlin compliant through threats, through a panicked atmosphere or through the difficulties created by a blockade. These forms of pressure will be rendered harmless if we maintain our courage. Thus, everything that gives citizens courage and confidence should be regarded positively. One way to strengthen our spiritual attitude is to make a celebratory pledge that we would rather go hungry than to give up our freedom. When a great number of Berlin citizens make this promise, a new atmosphere of power will be created in Berlin. Berlin has become a symbol for the entire world. The world already knows the courageousness of Berlin's citizens. And every further demonstration of spiritual power will fill people in other countries, who are also threatened by Communist tyranny and who are amazed by the courage of the Berliners, with confidence."[12]

Following the erection of the Berlin Wall, Zutshi planned what was perhaps his most spectacular demonstration on Gandhi's birthday, on October 2, 1962. The plan was announced to the public on September 30, 1962, in the student house on Steinplatz in West Berlin: together with Berthold Rubin, a history professor from Cologne, Zutshi wanted to break off pieces of the Wall along Bernauer Strasse with a hammer, chisel and crowbar. Zutshi's original plan was to continue these hammering actions every day at noon along different parts of the Berlin Wall. On September 12, 1962, he had already informed the West Berlin Police Chief Moch of his intentions in a letter. He had also written to the East German leader Walter Ulbricht: "I call upon you to shoot at me, just as you have so shamelessly shot at so many unarmed refugees."[13]

The East Berlin police built embrasures in the wall of a building located adjacent to the Reconciliation Church in order, according to East German sources, to prevent an "attack" from Zutshi, who was ostensibly "supported by espionage organizations."[14] The West Berlin police, for their part, feared that the West Berlin demonstrators would be seriously endangered in East Berlin. West Berlin Senator for the Interior Heinrich Albertz and the British, French and American commanders in West Berlin forbade Zutshi from breaking off pieces of the Wall. Despite this ban, which was announced by Albertz at a press conference, approximately 1000 Berlin citizens, primarily young people and students, gathered at the appointed time on Bernauer Strasse on October 2, 1962. The Berlin daily newspaper "Der Tagesspiegel" reported on the following day:

"Early Tuesday morning around 1 : 00 AM, Professor Rubin from Cologne began hammering the Wall with a chisel at the Reconciliation Church on Bernauer Strasse. However, before he was able to break off a piece of the Wall, he was stopped by a West Berlin police officer, who had rushed to the scene. Professor Rubin was first brought to the 52nd police precinct, and was then driven to his home by the Deputy Police Chief. Before his release, Professor Rubin had promised that he would undertake no further actions.

Yesterday at noon, the West Berlin police undertook comprehensive measures to prevent demonstrations on Bernauer Strasse. Six police vans with special police units, as well as several loudspeaker vans were stationed on Hussitenstrasse. The police pushed the crowd of people back onto the West Berlin side of the Wall. They even prevented West German students from unfolding a banner upon which a sentence from the Constitution of the Zone about freedom of movement was written. A supporter of Zutshi's, who had begun a sit-in in front of the Church of Reconciliation on Bernauer Strasse and wanted to remain there in prayer for three days and three nights, was taken into custody by the police.

On Tuesday morning, East Berlin officials sent in reinforcements on the border. As the Associated Press reported, the border guards placed heavy machine gun artillery in the bell tower of the Reconciliation Church, and reinforcements were positioned in the church tower. A water canon and a loudspeaker van were stationed behind the church. In the observation holes and skylights of East Berlin houses along the border, one could see the heads of the Pankow border guards. During the night, border guards had made a hole in the gable wall of the house on Bernauer Strasse 2 and placed an armored plate with a observation slit over it."[15]

One week later, 300 Berliners came together again with Zutshi and the well-known psychiatrist Dr. Wladimir Lindenberg,[16] a Russian emigrant, to participate in music and prayers beneath a large picture of Gandhi on the corner of Bernauer Strasse and Hussitenstrasse. The demonstrators were repeatedly disturbed by loud military marching music from loudspeakers in East Berlin. In the following weeks, however, the official resonance for these prayer sessions, which Zutshi held at various locations on Saturdays and Sundays from four o'clock in the afternoon to seven o'clock in the evening, decreased.

Discouraged by the increasing lack of support for his actions, and by the faint-heartedness and muteness of people in Berlin, who seemed to have resigned themselves to the Wall in their city, Zutshi decided to return to India in June 1964. Difficulties, which Zutshi had in finding satisfactory employment, may have also played a role in this decision. Zutshi had come to Germany with only a tourist visa. He did not have a work permit and thus encountered problems with the employment office as well as with immigration officials.[17] There were urgent appeals in press for Berlin entrepreneurs to offer Zutshi work, and he did for a time find employment as an unskilled laborer in the Berlin power plant Reuter. "I will not say that I am disappointed with this," Zutshi said about his decision to return home, "a freedom fighter cannot be disappointed. But given the present situation in Berlin, my time here would be wasted. … I am a poor man, but I will return again."[18]

We do not have any evidence as yet as to whether Zutshi actually did return to Berlin. What became of Zutshi and the "Satyagraha Society" in the years following would be but one of the many aspects which further research into the history of the Berlin Wall would bring to light.

4 Neues Deutschland, April 1, 1960
5 Der Abend, March 29, 1960
6 Der Abend, March 30, 1960
7 Die Zeit, April 8, 1960
8 Die Zeit, April 8, 1960
9 A letter from Zutshi from February 16, 1960
10 "Satyagraha in Berlin, by T.N. Zutshi," typed manuscript from 1960, p. 1
11 "Satyagraha in Berlin," p. 1
12 "Satyagraha in Berlin," p. 2, 3, 6
13 Berliner Morgenpost, September 19, 1962
14 National-Zeitung, October 3, 1962
15 Der Tagesspiegel, October 3, 1962
16 Telegraf, October 10, 1962
17 Der Tagesspiegel, June 24, 1960
18 Berliner Morgenpost, June 17, 1964

Despite the prohibition of the demolition protest, thousands of young West Berliners meet on Bernauer Strasse on October 2, 1962. They are pushed back by the West Berlin police

300 demonstrators gather in Bernauer Strasse to pray with Zutshi for the victims of the Wall

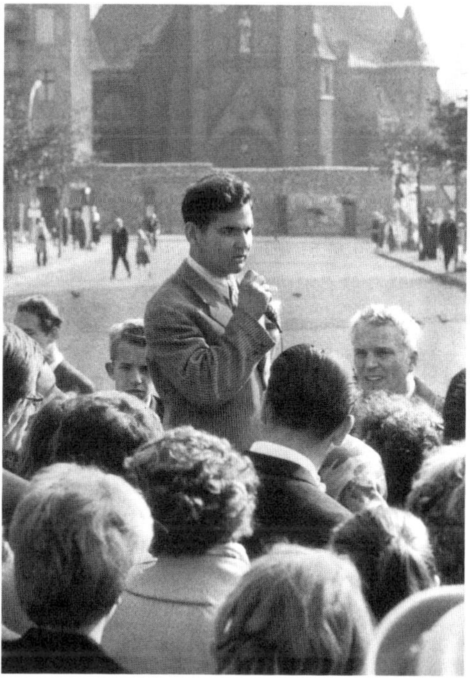

Zutshi before his trip to Berlin's East Sector on March 26, 1960

Zutshi (on the left in front of the picture of Gandhi) before a protest fast on Mariannenplatz in August 1963

Zutshi paddling in the East Berlin part of the Britz canal in the district Berlin-Neukölln to demonstrate for the refugee-helper Harry Seidel, sentenced to life imprisonment in the GDR

"I would not want to go through something like that again."

A Contemporary Witness Reports on his Experiences on Bernauer Strasse

On one of the first days of spring this year, I traveled to the outskirts of Berlin in order to talk to a contemporary witness of the Berlin Wall about his experiences. I was interested in how the division of the city had affected his life. Mr. Schirmer is one of the many people whose stories have not been told in the media. He greeted me in front of his house with the words, "I'm not at all sure that my life will be that interesting to you." This is what many contemporary witnesses of the Wall feel. They don't find their stories spectacular or earth-stattering, and they are not accustomed to talking about these difficult experiences, which are often completely ordinary, and yet at the same time, extraordinary as well. Conversations with contemporary witnesses are a significant source in understanding how historical events and political decisions affected the lives of individual people, and what alternatives of action were available to those people. The life stories of people directly affected by the Wall can also help to answer those questions which move us when we investigate the division of Berlin and Germany as a whole.

How did people experience the erection of the Wall? How did the Wall affect their lives? What motivated one person to try to escape, while another person chose to remain? In what ways did these decisions determine or change people's lives, and what did it mean for their family members, friends and neighbours? How did they react, and how did they deal with the pain? Where are the former border guards, and what do they think about what they did along the Wall? And what has become of those people in the Western part of the city who fought against the Wall?

These are some of the questions which visitors of the Memorial Site on Bernauer Strasse have posed when they have attempted to imagine the reality of the Wall dividing city, neighbourhood, family, friends and church parishes. The history of Mr. Schirmer and his wife, and those of other contemporary witnesses can help us answer such questions.

Karl-Heinz Schirmer, born in 1928, tells me thoughtfully about his life on and around Bernauer Strasse. "I grew up on Weinbergsweg on Rosenthaler Platz. My parents had a restaurant on Weinbergsweg. My first connection to Bernauer Strasse was through the Jungvolk.[19] Our troop had its meetings on Bernauer Strasse, in the school just in front of the current Memorial Site." Although Karl-Heinz Schirmer was subjected to a Nazi education in the Hitler Youth, he did not remain untouched by events in his neighbourhood. In his parents' restaurant, he encountered people with the most divergent political views, for among the restaurant guests were Nazis as well as Communists. He observed the heated discussions and political debates with keen interest, both in the restaurant and on the street. The violence against Jews in his neighbourhood was also no secret to the young boy, as his own uncle was Jewish. Mr. Schirmer remembers particularly clearly the visit from a Jewish school friend on the evening before the friend was deported. The helplessness he felt then is still evident today when he recalls the visit.

Like his contemporaries, Karl-Heinz Schirmer was drafted as an airforce helper in 1944 at the age of 16. His own family was greatly affected by the war. On February 25, 1945, his father was killed in an air raid. He was buried in the Sophien cemetery, next to the cemetery wall on Bernauer Strasse. His grave was part of the rows of War graves which would later lie in the immediate vicinity of the Berlin Wall. For the seventeen-year-old Karl-Heinz Schirmer, the loss of his father was particularly painful. The cemetery became an important site of remembrance and commemoration for the entire family. During their regular visits, the Schirmers were able to experience developments along the border first hand. After the building of the Wall, his father's grave was located in a part of the cemetery which was separated from the rest of the cemetery by a fence. The family was allowed to visit the grave only during set times of the day, and only with a permit and a 'grave card.' They were forced to watch as border soldiers with dogs patrolled between the graves and had to endure repeated identification checks. Even if they can no longer remember the exact dates when a particular fence was built or was altered, or when the barrier was put up so that cemetery visitors could no longer look into the "death strip" or Todesstreifen, their impressions and emotions from those times are still alive today.

The possibility of escaping from the Sophien cemetery to West Berlin made the border guards particularly watchful. Mr. Schirmer experienced this himself in 1976. On July 6 of that year, he happened to be in the neighbourhood. "As I approached the cemetery, I decided to go in and water by my father's grave. I did not have a watering can with me, so I took a large flowerpot and went back and forth, watering with it. About 15 minutes later, a henchman was standing next to me and asked to see my identification card and my grave card, which I didn't have with me. With this, I was already almost a 'border violator.' Now the torture started. The identification card checked out. Then they asked me about the grave stone, the dates, and I could tell them everything. We went to the cemetery office, as I had told them when my father was buried, and this had to be checked in a fat book. But they didn't give up. I was placed in a so-called 'taxi without door handles on the inside,' and was taken to the appropriate police precinct. The head of the precinct gave me a piece of paper and told me to write down what had happened." The officer then handed him over to the Transport Police on Magazinstrasse, as Mr. Schirmer worked for the railroad. "Here I was put in a room with no handle on the door and with bars on the windows. Now I was practically a dangerous criminal."

Mr. Schirmer was held by the police for hours. In the meantime, his wife had become quite worried. In the evening, a member of the

Transport Police came by and questioned her about the grave in the cemetery and about the grave card. Only after she confirmed her husband's account was Mr. Schirmer released. Instead of an apology, he had to speak with the cadre leadership at work and pay a fine of 30.75 Marks.

Many people experienced reprisals in their everyday lives similar to those of Mr. Schirmer and his wife. In their authentic reports about these experiences, the border regime's brutality and contempt for human life becomes clear. Every conversation with a contemporary witness is thus an important contribution to documenting the occurrences of the former dividing line between East and West, and in keeping alive the memory of those people directly affected.

19 The Jungvolk was the division of the Hitler Youth for boys between 10 and 14 years of age

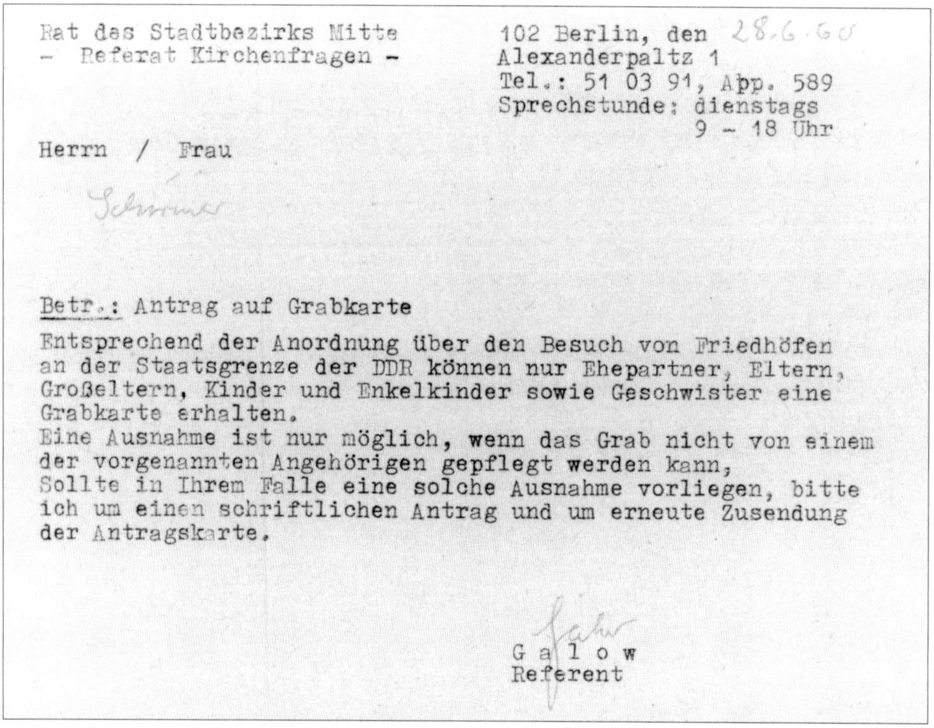

Rat des Stadtbezirks Mitte
- Referat Kirchenfragen -

102 Berlin, den 28.6.60
Alexanderpaltz 1
Tel.: 51 03 91, App. 589
Sprechstunde: dienstags
9 - 18 Uhr

Herrn / Frau

Schirmer

Betr.: Antrag auf Grabkarte

Entsprechend der Anordnung über den Besuch von Friedhöfen an der Staatsgrenze der DDR können nur Ehepartner, Eltern, Großeltern, Kinder und Enkelkinder sowie Geschwister eine Grabkarte erhalten.
Eine Ausnahme ist nur möglich, wenn das Grab nicht von einem der vorgenannten Angehörigen gepflegt werden kann,
Sollte in Ihrem Falle eine solche Ausnahme vorliegen, bitte ich um einen schriftlichen Antrag und um erneute Zusendung der Antragskarte.

G a l o w
Referent

Information about applying for a "grave card"

Pers.- Ausweis: ~~XV 030 ...~~
UVII-14-3
~~XV 125 40 86~~
XV 0820847
XV 0820848

Verwaltung
II. Sophien-Friedhof
Berlin N 4, Bergstr. 29

Bergstr.

Kirchhof der Sophien Kirchengemeinde

Name des Beerdigten: Margarete Schirmer

Tag der Beerdigung: 4. Oktober 1963

Bezeichnung der Grabstätte: V - 15 - 96

Diese Karte bitte bei Grabpflegebestellungen vorlegen.
Bei Wohnungswechsel des Grabpflegeberechtigten wird um Mitteilung gebeten.
Die Erwerber von Grabstellen sind den Bestimmungen der Kirchhofsordnung unterworfen.
Kurze Auszüge der Kirchhofsordnung befinden sich auf der Innenseite der Grabkarte.

Berlin, den 4. Oktober 191963
Fernsprecher: 424673

Verwaltung
II. Sophien Friedhof
Berlin N 4, Bergstr. 29

Die Kirchhofsverwaltung

D 2a

A "Grave card" for visiting the cemetery

Transportpolizei - Amt
Berlin
Dienststelle

Berlin, den 27 07 76 19

Nachweis-Nr.: 06053

Bei Einzahlungen und Nachfragen bitte volle Nachweis-Nr. angeben

Ordnungsstrafverfügung

Herrn / Frau / Frl. S c h i r m e r, Karl-Heinz geb. am 05. 03. 1928

wohnhaft 102 Berlin, Rochstraße 05 PA-Nr. XV 0820848

Sie haben am 06.07.1976 gegen 18.30 Uhr eine Ordnungswidrigkeit begangen, indem Sie durch Nichtbeachtung der für das Grenzgebiet der DDR festgelegten Aufenthaltsbestimmungen im Stadtbezirk Berlin-Mitte gegen die Sicherheit und Ordnung der Staatsgrenze verstoßen haben.

Ordnungswidrigkeit nach §§ 26(1) Grenzordnung v. 15.06.72 (GBL.II,S.483) 6(1) u. 7(1) Verordnung zum Schutze der Staatsgrenze v.19.03.64,i.d. Fassung v.11.09.75(GBL.I,Nr.38

Es wird daher gegen Sie als Ordnungsstrafmaßnahme

ein .... ausgesprochen*)

eine Ordnungsstrafe von 30,-- Mark (in Worten) - Dreißig - Mark festgesetzt*)

sowie .... verfügt.*)

Begründung: Sie haben sich auf dem Sophien-Friedhof in den als Grenzgebiet kenntlich gemachten Teil begeben, ohne im Besitz der dafür erforderlichen Genehmigung zu sein.

Zu den Ordnungsstrafmaßnahmen treten noch 0,75 Mark Auslagen.

Der Gesamtbetrag von 30,75 Mark ist innerhalb von 15 Tagen nach Zustellung dieser Ordnungsstrafverfügung an die Kasse der o. a. Dienststelle in der Zeit von - bis - Uhr außer .... einzuzahlen oder auf Konto Nr. .... der Industrie- und Handelsbank bzw. .... in .... zu überweisen.*)

Die anderen Ordnungsstrafmaßnahmen sind bis .... zu erfüllen.*)

Gegen diese Ordnungsstrafverfügung können Sie innerhalb von zwei Wochen Beschwerde bei der obigen Dienststelle einlegen. Die Beschwerde ist schriftlich einzulegen und zu begründen oder mündlich zu Protokoll zu erklären.

Diese Beschwerde hat .... aufschiebende Wirkung.

Wird innerhalb der gesetzten Frist bzw. nach Rechtskraft dieser Ordnungsstrafverfügung nicht nachgekommen, erfolgt die Beitreibung der Gesamtsumme bzw. die Durchsetzung der anderen Ordnungsstrafmaßnahmen.

Unterschrift / Dienststellung
Amtsleiter

*) Nichtzutreffendes ist zu streichen.

S 17 (87/11) Ag 106/2323/69

Karl-Heinz Schirmer's ticket for 30.75 Marks for visiting his father's grave without official permission

The GDR's National Day of Mourning in 1966 on the Sophien Cemetery. GDR border troops check the visitors' "grave cards"

In 1967, graves are reburied on the Sophien Cemetery in order to expand the border facilities

GROSS-BERLIN
RAT DES STADTBEZIRKS MITTE

Referat für Kirchenfragen
102 Berlin, den 18. Juli 1966

Sehr geehrte Frau Schirmer!

Betr.: Urnenstelle: **Martha Laabs**
Abt.: VII Reihe: 14 Nr.: 3

Wir möchten Sie davon unterrichten, daß im Interesse der Sicherheit auf dem Friedhof der evangelischen Sophienkirchengemeinde in der Bergstraße leider einige Veränderungen erforderlich sind.
Dazu gehört auch, daß die Urne Ihres Angehörigen umgesetzt werden muß. Die Urne wird auf einem Friedhof, den Sie uns benennen möchten, beigesetzt, da der Sophienfriedhof zur Zeit nur im geringen Maße aufnahmefähig ist. Es wird Ihnen eine Grabstelle in der gleichen Qualität zur Verfügung gestellt.

Zu etwaigen Rücksprachen innerhalb der Sprechstunden (dienstags von 9 - 18 Uhr) bin ich gern bereit.

Zur Klärung der neuen Urnenstelle möchte ich Sie bitten, sich mit der Verwaltung des jeweiligen von Ihnen gewünschten Friedhofes umgehend in Verbindung zu setzen, da die Umsetzungen in der nächsten Zeit erfolgen sollen.

Ich bitte um Ihr Verständnis für diese Maßnahme und um Ihre Unterstützung.

Hochachtungsvoll

G a l o w

Margarethe Schirmer was informed about the impending reburial of an aunt's urn in this letter from the GDR's Department for Church Questions

Chronology

of the Development of the Berlin Wall Memorial Site

March 1990
The directors of the Museum for German History (Berlin/GDR) and the German Historical Museum (West Berlin) write a joint letter to the German heads of state. In this letter, they recommend the construction of memorial site on the history of the Berlin Wall. For this purpose, they propose that an actual section of the border in the center of the city be protected as an historic monument. Bernauer Strasse is recommended as the location for this memorial site.

June 1990
The official demolition of the inner city Berlin Wall begins. Street connections between the East and West parts of the city are opened.

August 1990
The idea of a Wall memorial site is presented to the public for the first time at a press conference on the 29th anniversary of the building of the Wall. At this point in time, only an approximately 200-meter-long segment of the border is still available on Bernauer Strasse. This segment is part of the cemetery of the Sophien Parish in East Berlin between Ackerstrasse and Bergstrasse. During the press conference, the sisters of the Lazarus Hospital and Deaconess House stage a protest. With the assistance of the Federal Government, the German Historical Museum is able to prevent demolition of the border fortifications by GDR border troops.

October 1990
The municipal authorities in (East) Berlin designate the border segment on Bernauer Strasse as an historical monument. This decision is confirmed two years after German unification on February 6, 1992 by the first combined Berlin Senate.

August 1991
The Berlin Senate passes a resolution to erect a "commemoration and memorial site" on the occasion of the 30th anniversary of the building of the Wall. Following this, a heated debate begins in Berlin. The Sophien Parish and the Lazarus Hospital are resolutely opposed to the memorial site. The Reconciliation Parish on Bernauer Strasse, however, strongly supports the construction of a memorial site. The districts Berlin-Mitte and Berlin-Wedding react cautiously.

June 1992
The German Historical Museum assumes responsibility for ensuring the continued existence of the monument. Those directly af-

fected by the construction of the memorial site are brought together for a discussion. In this discussion, the basis for a design competition for the memorial is established. The Federal Government makes available the necessary funding. The Sophien Parish maintains its opposition to the memorial.

October 1992
As the legal successor to the East Berlin municipal authorities, the Land Berlin assumes responsibility for the border area in question. Until this time, the Federal Republic had been regarded as the legal successor. There are direct negotiations between the Land Berlin and the Sophien Parish concerning the realization of the memorial site project.

October 1993
The Land Berlin and the Sophien Parish reach an agreement in which the general conditions for the construction of a memorial site are established.

April/August 1994
The German Historical Museum sponsors a competition for the design of the Berlin Wall Memorial Site. 259 design proposals are accepted.

October 1994
There is no clear winner of the design competition. Three proposals are awarded second prize, and five additional proposals are also purchased.

July 1995
In agreement with the Land Berlin, the Federal Government chooses the proposal by the Architecture Office Kohlhoff & Kohlhoff from Stuttgart for the memorial site.

April 1997
Building Authorities Berlin-Mitte and the Sophien Parish arrange for the removal of 32 segments of the Wall in order to protect mass graves from the Second World War, which were ostensibly located beneath these Wall segments.

May/November 1997
Construction on the memorial site begins following the design proposal by Kohlhoff & Kohlhoff. The Land Berlin announces the construction of an Exhibition Center to supplement the memorial.

August 1997
Bishop Huber proposes an overall plan for the memorial site that includes a Monument, an Exhibition Center, and a "Chapel of Reconciliation."

August 1998
The memorial site officially opens on the anniversary of the erection of the Berlin Wall.

Die Authors

Professor Peter C. Bloth
Professor of Practical Theology and Campus Minister at the Humboldt University in Berlin

Dr. Gabriele Camphausen
Historian, Executive Director of the Foundation "Topography of Terror," and Chairwoman of "The Berlin Wall – Exhibition Center and Memorial Site" Association

Minister Manfred Fischer
Minister of the Evangelical Reconciliation Parish in Berlin-Wedding and a Member of the Executive Board of "The Berlin Wall – Exhibition Center and Memorial Site" Association

Doris Liebermann
Historian of Eastern Europe, Journalist, and Co-Worker of the Exhibition Center currently being constructed

Maria Nooke
Sociologist, Co-Worker of the Exhibition Center currently being constructed

Dr. Helmut Trotnow
Historian, Director of the Allied Museum, a Co-Worker at the German Historical Museum from 1990 to 1995, and an active participant in discussions on the construction of the Berlin Wall Memorial Site

Recommended Reading

Kai-Axel Aanderud/Guido Knopp (Ed.): Die eingemauerte Stadt: Die Geschichte der Berliner Mauer, Recklinghausen 1991

Polly Feversham and Leo Schmidt: Die Berliner Mauer heute, Denkmalswert und Umgang/The Berlin Wall Today, Cultural Significance and Conservation Issues, Berlin 1999

Peter Möbius/Helmut Trotnow: Mauern sind nicht für ewig gebaut. Zur Geschichte der Berliner Mauer, Berlin 1990

Peter Wyden: Die Mauer war unser Schicksal, Berlin 1995

Sources for the Illustrations

Archiv der Versöhnungsgemeinde: p. 17 l., 23, 25 top, 43, 45 top
Bundesarchiv Koblenz: p. 17 r. (183/1990/0613/423)
Theo Heimann: p. 45 bottom
Christian Jungebloth: p. 26 bottom
Landesbildstelle Berlin: p. 13 top, 16 top, 31 top, 32 bottom, 33, 42
Karl-Heinz Schirmer: p. 56, 57, 59
Günter Schneider: p. 6, 16 bottom., 44 bottom
Helmut Trotnow: p. 17 top, 24
Ullstein Bilderdienst: p. 13 bottom, 14/15 (Otto Stark), 25 bottom (Buddy Bartelsen), 26 top (Christian Bach), 31 bottom (Alex Waidmann), 32 top (Peter Leibing), 44 top (Günter Peters), 51 top (Pressefoto Schirmer), 51 l. (Heinz O. Jurisch), 51 r., 52top (AP), 52 bottom (AP), 58 top (Klaus Lehnartz), 58 bottom (Heinz O. Jurisch)